HANNIBAL THE CANNIBAL

HANNIBAL THE CANNIBAL

THE TRUE STORY OF ROBERT MAUDSLEY

ALAN R. WARREN

COPYRIGHT

HANNIBAL THE CANNIBAL: The True Story of Robert Maudsley
Written by Alan R. Warren

Published in Canada

Copyright @ 2020 by Alan R. Warren

All rights reserved. No part of this book may be reproduced, scanned, or distributed in any printed or electronic form without permission of the author. The unauthorized reproduction of a copyrighted work is illegal. Criminal copyright infringement, including infringement without monetary gain, is investigated by the FBI and is punishable by fines and federal imprisonment. Please do not participate in or encourage privacy of copyrighted materials in violation of the author's rights. Purchase only authorized editions.

This is a work of nonfiction. No names have been changed, no characters invented, no events fabricated.

Cover design, formatting, layout, and editing by Evening Sky Publishing Services

BOOK DESCRIPTION

Robert Maudsley casually walked into the cell of another inmate, who was sleeping on his bunk face down. A savage rage quickly took over, and Maudsley started stabbing the back of the man's head. There was blood, pieces of brain, and chunks of hair flying in a fury. After the man went limp, Maudsley grabbed the man's head and held it in both palms and started to smash it against the walls of the cell, so hard that the plaster began to fall off the ceiling.

Nurses and guards had to watch on, not being able to get into the cell, hearing the victim's head crack each time it was smashed against the wall. After Maudsley finished with the attack, he sat the limp body up against the bed, got down on his knees, and started to eat chunks of the brain with his home-made knife.

Robert Maudsley was dubbed "Hannibal the Cannibal" on account of his thirst for eating the brains of his victims. He is one of the most interesting and thought provoking murderers in prison. He will be housed in a bulletproof cage, in the basement of Wakefield Prison, England, where

Britain hold its most savage, high profile convicts. He is known to be such a danger to others, even inmates, he lives in a specially designed cell that doesn't allow him any contact with anybody, except for guards that will slide his food through a small hole at the bottom of one of his cells.

Robert Maudsley is deemed to be the "Most Dangerous Prisoner in Britain." Even though he only killed one person outside of prison, his remaining victims were claimed while incarcerated. This book reviews Maudsley's life from his tormented childhood, his rage-filled murder outside of prison, and the planned torturous murders of three convicted pedophiles.

In the basement of Wakefield, you might be surprised who else has been housed beside Maudsley, and what kind of relationship they have.

CONTENTS

Introduction ix

1. Morning Has Broken 1
2. Murder of John Farrell 5
3. Hospital Murder of David Francis 11
4. Murders in Prison 15
5. Solitary Confinement 21
6. "Monster Mansion" 29
7. Letter to The Times UK 55
   Epilogue 63

About the Author 69
Also By 71
References 75

INTRODUCTION

"It does not matter to them whether I am mad or bad. They do not know the answer, and they do not care, just so long as I am kept out of sight and out of mind." - Robert Maudsley

Robert Maudsley, dubbed "Britain's most dangerous prisoner," has been imprisoned for more than 40 years, even though he has not committed any crimes in the last 25 of those years. He is considered so dangerous that he has been in solitary confinement for more than 30 years, with no chance of getting out until his death.

Maudsley has been the owner of several nicknames over the years he has been in prison. First, he was called "Blue" because that was the color of his first victim's face when he slowly strangled him to death. Later, he became known as "Spoons" because his second victim's body was found with a spoon sticking out of its head, and some of the brain missing. However, it was Maudsley's third and fourth victims, killed on the same day, that earned him the nickname he carries today "Hannibal the Cannibal."

When the name "Hannibal the Cannibal" is mentioned, we think of Sir Anthony Hopkins in the 1991 movie *The Silence of the Lambs* or perhaps one of the many other films in the series. Everyone thinks they know who Hannibal is, what drove him to kill and eat his victims, where he lived, or how he lived his life. Similar to people thinking they know Robert Maudsley. However, the truth is never as straight forward as it seems.

As with all things in life, there are always two sides to the story. Robert Maudsley's friends and family describe him as gentle, kind, and highly intelligent. They enjoy his sense of humor and company. Maudsley has a genius-level IQ, loves classical music, poetry, and art. And he is excited to be taking an Open University degree in Music theory.

Maudsley's brother claims that the prison authorities are trying to break him. Every time they see he is making a little progress, they throw a wrench in the works. There was a point while he was in Woodhill Prison, where he was reported to be making great progress. Even to the extent that he was able to play chess with a group of prison guards, listen to music, and read books. Despite the fact that Maudsley was doing well, the prison authorities decided to move him back to Wakefield Prison and put him in a specially constructed glass cage for a cell.

The notorious UK criminal Charles Bronson wrote a book in 2007 called *Loonyology*, in which he claims he saw 'Bob' (Robert Maudsley) go mad, and he knew what was happening to him. Bronson also claims that when Maudsley went for his one hour of exercise each day, he was put outside in the 20 by 12-foot prison yard by himself, as he wasn't allowed any contact with other prisoners. Maudsley was seen pacing around the yard with his eyes fixed on the ground and sporting a very long grey beard and nails.

One of Maudsley pen pal friends who came to see him in prison said that she found him very friendly:

> "Everyone is concentrating on the crimes he did 25 years ago as if they are in a time loop, and no one is prepared to look at him now."

This book is one in a series of short books covering some of the most shocking serial killers. As with all true crime accounts, it starts by gathering as much of the pertinent information of the case available at the time of writing. In the case of older serial killers that committed their crimes in the 1960s and 1970s, a lot of the witnesses and people involved are long gone or passed away. But quite often, we are left with various written witness accounts about the way the serial killer behaved both in and out of prison.

While examining many letters and communications with professionals who had contact with serial killer Robert Maudsley, I found a particular professional's response to him far different than any other.

Paul Harrison is a former police detective with over 40 years of experience in the British justice system. He is known as the "British Mindhunter." Harrison has met and interviewed some of the world's most notorious criminals, and with over 25 years of profiling serial killers, he is able to provide real details rather than myths that surround them.

According to Harrison's report in *The Manchester Evening News*, when he sat down with Robert Maudsley for an interview, he found him to be surprisingly approachable. Harrison says:

> "These criminals have done some really bad things, and 99.99% of them deserve to be where they are, but there are always some that make you think. One of those was Maudsley, who was actually determined to be interviewed by me."

Maudsley once stated:

> "You've got the image of a monster. A horrible, evil man."

But Harrison commented that when they were communicating, he could understand why he did what he did:

> "If you didn't know him and what he'd done, and you saw him in a bar, he's really intelligent, clever guy who made you smile. He talks about everyday things. A lot of serial killers are really intense and

narcissistic and talk about themselves, and I didn't find that at all (with Maudsley)."

Harrison reports that Maudsley is the only serial killer where he actually thought:

"Wow, this is something different from any serial killer, Maudsley is different.

He doesn't want to get out of prison. He's been in there too long. His issues are more about getting equal treatment with other prisoners, getting some fresh air. But because he's a special category and a danger to society, it's like he's become a legend, even in the prison system."

Harrison even admitted feeling real empathy for Maudsley, even though he killed two pedophiles. He claims there are people worse than Maudsley in the prison system who have gotten away with a lot more. Harrison wrote to the Home Secretary and even the Queen and anybody else he could think of but received no responses.

Throughout this book, you will see more opinions like this, where the most frequent questions I am asked about Maudsley is

1. Did he really eat somebody else's brains?
2. Should he be treated the way he is, being in solitary confinement, for over 30 years, without

any communication with others? After all, he
only killed pedophiles.

By the end of this book, I think you'll be asking more about how the criminal justice system works in such a complex case.

1

MORNING HAS BROKEN

Toxteth area of Liverpool, England is in the south part of the city center and is primarily residential with old terraced-houses, and World War II social housing, Victorian in style. Toxteth has been a popular place for immigrants from Africa, China, India, Yemen, and Somalia to relocate.

The economic decline after World War II left Toxteth, and all of Liverpool, with some of the highest unemployment in the country. This area of England is best known for the famous band, the Beatles. Not only did they start out there, playing a lot of clubs, but Ringo Starr was born there, and John Lennon's family lived there for years.

Robert Maudsley was born in Toxteth, Liverpool, in June of 1953 and was one of twelve children. There isn't a lot known of Maudsley's early life, but we do know that his father was a truck driver providing for his wife and four children. By the time Robert was two-years old, he and his brothers, Paul and Kevin, and sister Brenda were all taken into care by child protection for parental neglect.

Paul and Kevin were sent to Nazareth House, a Catholic orphanage in Liverpool, and Robert was sent to the Catholic orphanage in Crosby, Merseyside. After six years, their parents took them back home to reunite with the latest siblings of their growing family.

Robert's brother Paul later commented,

> "At the orphanage, we had all got on really well. Then our parents would come to visit, but they were just strangers. The nuns were our family, and we all used to stick together. Then our parents took us home, and we were subjected to physical abuse. It was something we never experienced before. They just picked on us, one by one, gave us a beating, and sent us off to our room."

Robert Maudsley was taken back from the orphanage when he was only eightyears-old. He claimed:

> "All I remember of my childhood is the beatings. Once I was locked in a room for six months, and my father only opened the door to come in to beat me four to six times a day. He used to hit me with a stick or a rod and even once hit me with his .22 caliber rifle."

Later in his life, Robert also claimed that his father raped him.

The details aren't known, but Social Services took Robert from his parents again, and he was placed in a series of foster homes from then on. His father told the rest of the kids that Robert died, so he was never visited by any of them during this time.

At the age of 16, Robert drifted to London. He began using street drugs, and over the next few years, checked himself into rehab several times.

Robert was working as a 'rent boy' (male prostitute for other men) to support himself and his drug habit. He met many men over this time, most of them he wouldn't remember as he was so high while having sex with them.

Robert attempted suicide at least three times during this period and was placed in psychiatric hospitals. He told the doctors he was hearing voices in his head that told him he needed to go home and kill his parents.

| *Robert Maudsley at the orphanage*

2

MURDER OF JOHN FARRELL

John Farrell was a laborer, and in 1973, he lived on a farm on the outskirts of town. He enjoyed the privacy and serenity the farm and several animals created. He was previously married, but his wife couldn't adapt to the country lifestyle, so she ended up leaving him and moving back to the city.

Farrell didn't fight too hard to keep his wife. In the back of his mind, a secret was slowly showing itself more every day. He had an affection towards other men. He enjoyed being around them and was very comfortable having sex with them too. Now that his wife was gone, he was free to go out to the area where 'rent boys' would be waiting to be bought for the night. And with her gone, he was free to take his rent boy back to his house, instead of having uncomfortable sex in his car.

Farrell wanted to find a 'regular.' A friend with benefits. Someone he didn't have to pay for. But that was very difficult for a rough laborer to do. So, he went to the street in London and picked up someone who looked halfway clean and, hopefully, was not a drug addict. It was during one of these trips that he met and picked up Robert Maudsley.

Farrell really liked Maudsley as he fit his style for looks and body type, was clean, very polite and easy to talk to. The only issue he had was that Maudsley liked to do drugs. All sorts of drugs, and all the time when they were together for sex. Their relationship went on for about 5 or 6 months.

About the tenth date with Maudsley, Farrell figured it was time to experiment a little further with his sexuality. He had another secret longing he wanted Maudsley to know about. And he was hoping Robert would join him in fulfilling that desire. Farrell took Maudsley back to his house like the other times, where they both got undressed, laid on the bed, and started to make out.

Within five minutes, Farrell got up, went to his dresser, opened a drawer, and pulled out some pictures. He came back to the bed where Maudsley was so high he didn't even notice Farrell had left and said:

"Hey, I want you to look at something."

Maudsley hardly moved and just groaned.

Farrell said loudly:

"Hey, boy, take a look!"

Maudsley pulled himself up and sat with his back against the headboard, mumbling:

"What?"

Farrell asked, "These pictures. Look at them. They are great. They really get me going. Don't you like nude pictures of boys?"

Maudsley answered, "Sure, sure I do, why not?"

He grabbed the pictures from Farrell and placed them on the bed in front of himself saying, "What are these?"

With an evil grin on his face, Farrell said, "There some nice little boys that did what their daddy told them to do. They did what I wanted them to do. Those little bitches took my cock real nice, like your (sic) going to do."

Maudsley was going through the pictures, while his drug-addled brain began to process what they were. He saw that they were pictures of little boys or very young men. He kept shuffling through them, not really listening to what Farrell was saying. He slowly started going into what he later described as a 'fog.'

Farrell shouted, "Hey! Are you listening to me, boy? Boy!"

All Maudsley could see was the pain and fear in the faces of the boys in the pictures. This triggered his memories of being eight-years-old, his father coming into his bedroom, snapping his belt loudly, pushing him down onto the bed, and ripping the pants off him with such anger. Robert remembered how his father slowly entered him from behind, and no matter how many times he screamed, his father kept thrusting. After his father finished in Robert, he pulled out, and he could feel blood running out of his ass.

Suddenly, Robert felt a slap across his face, "I said, do you fucking hear me, boy?"

Maudsley quickly got out of the bed and yelled, "What, what do you want?"

Farrell scooted up on the bed and rolled around until he was lying face up and looked at Maudsley, "I want you to do as your told like you were one of those boys in the pictures."

Maudsley backed his way towards the bedroom door, not sure what he was going to do. He noticed what looked like a rope tied into a noose sitting on top of a chair in the bedroom. Slowly, he walked toward the chair and grabbed the rope. On the floor were some wooden hangers. He picked one up and said, "I'm going to give you what you deserve."

And he smiled with the same evil grin Farrell wore when they first got into bed.

With an excited laugh, Farrell asked, "Oh yeah?"

Maudsley answered, "Yeah."

Then he suddenly jumped on top of Farrell, who was still lying flat on the bed. Maudsley adjusted himself, so he was sitting directly on Farrell's stomach. He quickly looped the rope around Farrell's neck, and stuck one arm of the hanger in between the rope and his neck and started twisting the hanger.

Realizing quickly that this was not a sexual game, Farrell began to fight. He tried to grab the rope and hanger, but Maudsley's rage had taken over, and he was too strong. With both hands, Maudsley continued to twist no matter how hard Farrell fought. Soon, Farrell ran out of oxygen and started to get dizzy, and Maudsley suddenly stopped twisting. He brought himself so that he was face to face with Farrell.

Farrell was still alive, but his face was turning a bluish color. Maudsley looked directly into his eyes and said, "Was this what you wanted, daddy?"

He twisted the hanger one more time, and Farrell passed out. He held the hanger with a hard grip for at least two minutes before finally letting it go.

Maudsley was later arrested and charged with the

murder of John Farrell. After the court evaluated him and his history of abuse, several attempted suicides, and hearing voices in his head, they sentenced him to a life sentence to be served in the Broadmoor Hospital for the Criminally Insane.

3

HOSPITAL MURDER OF DAVID FRANCIS

Maudsley would not last long in Broadmoor Hospital. Once Maudsley got a taste of violence with Farrell, a well opened up inside him.

In 1977, he and another inmate, David Cheeseman, forcibly grabbed a third inmate, David Francis, a convicted pedophile who had previously raped a friend of theirs and dragged him kicking and screaming across the corridor, towards Maudsley's cell. Four nurses tried to stop them but were threatened by Maudsley and Cheeseman with knives made from parts of a dismantled radio.

Instead of going all the way to Maudsley's cell, they dragged Francis into the first office that had an open door. Cheeseman tied Francis up with some wire from a record player. For more than nine hours, the prison witnessed the agonizing screams from Francis as Maudsley and Cheeseman tortured him. Later, staff described hearing Francis scream out, "God, no, God, no!"

They were punching, kicking, and cutting his body with their prison-made knives.

Just after 8 p.m., the nurses and other prisoners said the screaming stopped. Maudsley had garroted Francis to death. Maudsley and Cheeseman then lifted the body of David Francis above their heads and moved it so that the guards and nurses could see it through the window of the office door. After allowing the body to be viewed for a few minutes, Maudsley unlocked the door.

The guards rushed into the office to contain the scene, and soon after, two nurses came in to check on Francis. One of the guards claimed that the dead man's head was cracked open like a boiled egg. A spoon was hanging out of his head, and a large part of his brain was gone. They believed it was Maudsley who took his spoon and sampled Francis' brain. How much was actually eaten was unknown.

Broadmoor Hospital for the Criminally Insane

Most of the nine-hour attack was witnessed by several inmates, prison guards, and a nurse. The reason why they were not able to stop the attack was unknown. It was reported that at the time of the attack, the nurses and guards were unarmed, locked in a cell, and Maudsley had jammed the lock. However, it is questionable that it would take them nine hours to get the required help to a prison hospital to stop such a brutal attack.

Ironically, even though this murder occurred in an insane asylum, Maudsley was considered fit to stand trial in a regular criminal court.

The two men were charged with manslaughter, and both were sentenced to life in prison with no chance for parole.

Maudsley was moved to a Category A prison (a prison for dangerous offenders with a high probability of escape) to serve out his new sentence. He hated the regular style of prison and petitioned to be moved back to the Broadmoor hospital, but was denied.

By the time Maudsley arrived at Wakefield Prison, his new nickname was "Spoons," and the reason for that was obvious. The spoon in the brain was never confirmed by any media sources; however, it originated from the witnesses at the prison.

| *Wakefield Prison Outside View*

| Wakefield Prison Inside View

Maudsley had now murdered two people; both of them convicted child molesters. Because of that fact, people didn't seem to be upset about it. In fact, most admitted they were glad the world had two fewer molesters. The only problem the public had was that the second killing involved eating the victim's brains with a spoon.

Murder UK received a letter from one of the prison guards at the Broadmoor Hospital. The guard claimed in his letter that the inmates were only allowed plastic cutlery, and only a fork and spoon, no knife. In regular prisons, inmates would also have a plastic knife. The guard also claimed that Maudsley had created a makeshift weapon by snapping the blade of a spoon down the middle to create a roughly pointed weapon.

4

MURDERS IN PRISON

A mere few months later, at Wakefield Prison, Maudsley decided to go on a rampage intending to kill as many inmates on the same afternoon as he could. He figured that if he killed a few men this time, they would deem him insane and send him back to Broadmoor Hospital.

In July 1978, shortly before his morning exercise time, Maudsley stood behind the door of his cell, holding his prison-made knife crafted from a canteen soup spoon. He had certain inmates in mind to kill, and anybody that had sexually assaulted children was first on his list. But any sexual deviant would do.

Maudsley recalled all the years of abuse he dealt with as a child, the longing inside him to kill his parents for it, and the loss at never having the opportunity. This was his way of making up for that loss. If he couldn't kill his parents, he would kill others that committed the same crime and got away with it. In Maudsley's mind, being put in prison was, in fact, getting away with the crime.

Finally, he saw one of his chosen inmates - Salney Darwood, a 46-year-old sex offender who was convicted and sentenced to life in Wakefield Prison for the manslaughter of his wife. The two had met a few weeks earlier as Darwood was giving French language class to inmates, and Maudsley was one of his students.

Maudsley invited Darwood back to his cell. Whether he had to offer him drugs or sex to get him to agree was unknown. As Darwood entered the cell, Maudsley quickly jumped out behind him and started frenziedly stabbing him in the back, neck, and head. With no warning of Maudsley's intent, his victim soon fell to the floor, bleeding, and rolled onto his back. Maudsley quickly got onto his knees and stabbed Darwood in the chest, face, and neck until he knew he was dead.

To ensure Darwood was dead, he grabbed some string he had hidden under his mattress pad and tied it around his neck, holding it tight for several minutes. Maudsley tied the string into a bow and rolled Darwood's body under his bunk. He then washed his hands as well as he could before heading back out into the general population.

Maudsley slowly worked his way out to the yard, with his knife tucked into the waistband of his prison trousers. He talked to other inmates while searching for his next victim. It took him just over an hour before spotting him, William Roberts. Roberts was perfect. Maudsley never met him before but knew him from reputation – as a child molester.

Fifty-six-year-old William Roberts was lying face down on his bed, catching an afternoon nap. He crept into Roberts' cell, slowly and quietly enough so that Roberts didn't hear him. He stood over Roberts for a moment and then suddenly started to stab viciously at the back of his head. Quickly, Roberts turned over, and as soon as his eyes met Maudsley's, the stabbing stopped.

Roberts placed his arms in front of his face in a defensive position, asking what the hell was going on. Maudsley grinned widely and chuckled while continuing to stab Roberts in the chest, arms, and face. Within minutes, Roberts' arms fell to his side, and his body went limp. Maudsley threw his knife to the floor and dragged the lifeless body from the bed. He grabbed Roberts' head with both hands and smashed it against the wall with such force you could hear the skull cracking with each hit.

The scene looked like a bird trying to get out of a room from where it was trapped hitting every wall, the floor, and even the ceiling in its fury. Each time Roberts' skull was smashed, another piece of brain matter loosened and fell to the floor. Maudsley was so caught up in the attack he wouldn't stop until there was almost no skull left in his hands, only soft and wet brain matter. When he finally dropped what was left of his victim's head on the floor, it sounded sloppy like the dropping of cooked pasta. By the end of the attack, there were over 40 stab wounds throughout the body. Or at least that was what they could count. In reality, Roberts' face and head were so destroyed that there was no way to tell precisely how many times he had been stabbed.

Maudsley proceeded to wipe off as much of the blood from his hands as he could, on Roberts' pants. He took the knife and walked into the guard's office and placed it on the table, saying:

"It looks like you'll be short two on roll call."

He was giving himself up, all while wearing a broad smile. The guards saw that both the knife and Maudsley's prison uniform were covered in blood. Two of the guards cuffed him, while several others ran towards Roberts' cell.

In a matter of minutes, the first guards reached the cell. But they quickly stopped when realizing the floor was so covered in blood, brain matter, and plaster from the walls, that they couldn't walk in without contaminating the scene.

Darwood's body was later found under the bed in Maudsley's cell. Maudsley was arrested and placed in solitary confinement and charged with two counts of murder.

Robert Maudsley was now known as "Britain's most dangerous prisoner."

During the murder trial, Maudsley admitted that during his violent rages, he imagined his victims were his mother and father. His lawyers argued the murders were a result of pent-up aggression resulting from his terrible childhood.

Murder UK received another letter from a Wakefield prison guard, who claimed to be on duty the Saturday Maudsley killed his two victims. He said Maudsley created another makeshift knife from a plastic spoon, just as he did in Broadmoor Hospital. He took the weapon and plunged it into the ear of his first victim, Darwood. It was when he pulled it out of the victim's ear, that brain matter had spattered all over the cell floor and wall. The guard claimed that none of it was ever eaten by Maudsley.

The guard also claimed that after his second victim, Roberts, was dead, Maudsley started swinging his body around the cell, hitting the victim's head on the cell walls. That's why it was described in court that Maudsley smashing Robert's head was like breaking eggshells.

The prison guard's letter was problematic. How was it that he was able to not only describe what happened in one of the killings but both? Was he watching them? And if he was watching both murders, why didn't he try to stop it, and call other officers to help? None of what he claimed made sense. Unless, he was happy about the murders, or maybe even behind them.

When Maudsley was sentenced to life in prison the first time, it gave him an invisible license to kill in prison. Maudsley was convicted of the double murders in a regular criminal court. He was sentenced to two more life terms to be served in prison, not a hospital. Maudsley's plan had failed. He appealed the sentence but lost his appeal.

Following sentencing, Maudsley was sent to Parkhurst Prison on the Isle of Wight in early 1980. There, he ended up staying for three years and was able to work with the prison psychiatrist, Dr. Bob Johnson, who came to believe that Maudsley was making progress at controlling his anger and depression. According to Dr. Johnson, Maudsley made significant progress and was three-quarters of the way through removing the aggression and latent violence that made him a dangerous person.

Unfortunately, his treatment was discontinued in 1983 when Maudsley was suddenly and unexpectedly sent back to Wakefield Prison. Dr. Johnson was upset that without notice, prison authorities moved Maudsley back to Wakefield, and he was forced to stop treatment. Wakefield decided to put him into a special cell in solitary confinement. He was confined to his new specially-built cell for ten years. Then he moved again to Woodhill Prison near Milton Keynes. The prison system built him another special cell in their solitary confinement wing and placed Maudsley there.

SOLITARY CONFINEMENT

"The prison authorities see me as a problem, and their solution has been to put me in solitary confinement and throw away the key, to bury me alive in a concrete coffin. I am left to stagnate, vegetate, and to regress. Left to confront my solitary head-on with people who have eyes but don't see, and who have ears but don't hear, who have mouths but don't speak. My life in solitary is one long period of unbroken depression." - Robert Maudsley

These are the things that Maudsley has said for years, but recently a group of new supporters has formed. The internet has allowed these supporters to become a group or club, and they rally to give Maudsley a voice.

They claim that Maudsley has been the victim of an uncaring and unsympathetic prison system that virtually denies him treatment and does nothing to assist in his rehabilitation. For years, Maudsley has been and still is kept in a glass-like cage, a two-cell unit at Wakefield Prison like the one featured in *The Silence of the Lambs* movie. Perhaps that was where the makers of the movie got the idea, as Maudsley's cage was built in 1983, seven years before that movie's debut.

The two-cell unit that Maudsley calls home is 5.5 meters by 4.5 meters, which is slightly larger than the regular-sized cell of 4 meters by 4 meters in the UK. The cell unit has a bulletproof window made from Perspex (a transparent thermoplastic shatter-resistant alternative to glass) on all sides, so Maudsley can always be observed and have nowhere to hide.

The only furnishings are a plain table and one chair, which are both made from pressed cardboard. His cell sits over a cement slab, and the toilet and sink are both bolted to the slab. Quite often, the toilet backs up and smells like a sewer. The cell's cage is made from solid steel and has a small slot near the bottom of one side, where the guards pass food to the prisoner.

Maudsley spends 23 hours a day in his cell every day, with one hour permitted for exercise. He is escorted to the yard by no less than six prison guards and is not allowed contact with any of the other prisoners. This level of isolation is not imposed on any other prisoner.

The years in solitary confinement have taken its toll on Maudsley, who reportedly looks at least 20 years older than his actual age. It's said that when you first see him, you are mildly shocked at his deathly pale skin from the lack of any natural lighting or the sun. His skin is so transparent you can see his cheekbones through it. His hair is long, greasy, very unhealthy looking, and he has a grey beard.

When Maudsley was removed from Parkhurst Prison and send back to Wakefield, Maudsley's brother Paul commented in *The Daily Mirror*:

> "As far as I can tell, the prison authorities are trying to break him. Every time they see him making a little progress, they throw a spanner in the works. He spent time in Woodhill Prison, and there he was getting on well with the staff, even playing chess with them. He had access to books and music and television. Now they have put him back in the cage at Wakefield. His trouble started because he got locked up as a kid. All they do when they put him back there is bring all that trauma back to him."

Maudsley himself claims,

> "All I have to look forward to is further mental breakdown and possible suicide. In many ways, I think this is what the authorities hope for. That way, the problem of Robert John Maudsley can be easily and swiftly resolved."

Jane Heaton began to write Maudsley about three years ago:

> "Since getting to know Maudsley, I have seen many prison documents about him. Everyone concentrates on the crimes he committed 25 years ago. It's as if they are living in a time loop, and no one is prepared to look at how he is now. I would like to see him get an independent review of his condition and find a suitable course of treatment for him."

According to the Prison Authority, Maudsley has a problem that cannot be solved in any other way than exceptional confinement, given the outstanding danger he presents to other prisoners he may meet.

Professor Andrew Coyle, a professor of Prison Studies at the University of London and former prison governor, said people don't really understand what 'throw away the key' means. In a 2014 speech, he quoted from a United Nations report to the General Assembly that:

> "Prison regimes of solitary confinement often cause mental and physical suffering or humiliation that amounts to cruel, inhuman, or degrading treatment or punishment. Solitary confinement should be imposed, if at all, in very exceptional circumstances, as a last resort, for as short a time as possible."

Coyle went on to use an example from when he was a governor at a prison in Scotland:

> "In 1970, Thomas McCullough had been convicted of murdering two people and was ordered to be detained indefinitely in the Scottish Secure Psychiatric Hospital. In 1976, McCullough and another patient broke out of prison armed with an axe and knife. In the course of their escape, they killed another patient, a member of the nursing staff, and a policeman."

When they were both caught, both men were sentenced to life imprisonment, where McCullough was kept in a specially constructed suite of three rooms, a cell where he slept at night, a living area, and a workroom. The prison guard was present within the unit and directly always supervised his movements.

At the outset, Coyle said that it seemed like McCullough would never be released, but as the years passed and prison staff worked with him so successfully, he was eventually transferred to a lower security prison, and by 2013 McCullough was released from prison entirely. McCullough will remain under supervision where he lives for the rest of his life.

Professor Coyle was convinced that life imprisonment without a possibility of parole could benefit from the same treatment that McCullough had received but knows that there will be people against such an idea.

One of the biggest problems with applying this sort of

treatment to Maudsley is the reputation that he has as a 'brain eater' or 'cannibal.' The legend that has grown around his name will now stay with him until his death, even with a reasonable doubt as to whether he ate any brain or not. According to one of the prison guards that worked with Maudsley for over 20 years, "The reality is that Maudsley did no such thing."

However, Norman Brennan of the Victims of Crime Trust says:

> "Maudsley forfeited his right to be treated like other prisoners when he murdered three of his fellow inmates. Maudsley is a psychopath. He is a danger to everyone he comes into contact with, and we should not be bending over backward and spending unnecessary time and resources pandering to his every wish."

SOLITARY CONFINEMENT | 27

Pictures of Robert Maudsley's Cage in Solitary

"MONSTER MANSION"

Wakefield Prison is a Category A men's prison located in Wakefield, West Yorkshire, England. It is the largest high-security prison in the UK. The prison has been nicknamed "Monster Mansion" due to a large number of high-profile, high-risk sex offenders and murderers housed there - over 700 inmates, 600 of them convicted sex-offenders.

The solitary confinement wing is saved for the most notorious of the criminals locked up in Wakefield. They are the only ones able to see and have any possible contact with Maudsley.

The closest to him is a duplicate cell structure meant for another 'most dangerous' of inmates.

Below are the high-profile prisoners that were housed in the cage beside Maudsley for some of their time behind bars.

CHARLES BRONSON

Charles Bronson Salvador being led into a prison

Charles Bronson is a notorious prisoner who has been incarcerated for over 44 years of his life. Some refer to him as the "most violent prisoner in Britain." Most violent or not, he is undoubtedly one of the highest profile criminals. Some of his time in prisons has been spent in Wakefield alongside Robert Maudsley. They have a complicated relationship.

On November 14, 2017, during one of his brief stints *outside* the UK's many prisons, Bronson married a television actress Paula Williamson, known for roles on *Coronation Street* and *Emmerdale*. During the wedding, there were several pictures taken but never released to Bronson or his new wife. A short few months later, Bronson was back on the inside, and in January 2018, attempted to cause bodily harm to the governor of Wakefield prison, Mark Docherty. Before guards could restrain him, Bronson managed to threaten to bite off his nose and gouge out the governor's eyes. Bronson claims that he merely gave the governor a gentle bear hug and whispered to him, "Where's my wife's photos?"

Fully aware of who Robert Maudsley was and his intellect, Bronson, after his arrest, wanted Maudsley to defend him in the trial. He also wanted Maudsley to testify what 40 years in prison can do to a person.

After spending so much time in Wakefield Prison, and solitary confinement specifically after his frequent violent outbursts, Bronson had the opportunity to know Maudsley for many years. According to Bronson, Maudsley should be in a hospital instead of prison:

> "Did you see him outside, walking around? He's totally mad. He should be back in Broadmoor."

Maudsley has often been compared to the movie *The Silence of the Lambs*, pacing around his yard, staring at the ground, wearing a long, grey beard with a stooped figure. Bronson continued:

> "I know about Bob. I've seen him go mad; I know what's happened to him. But we hate each other now."

It turns out the two cons are sworn enemies after falling out over a Seiko watch Bronson had offered Maudsley. Maudsley refused the watch and told a prison officer to throw it away.

Bronson, who refers to this feud in his new book *Loonyology*, says:

> "I then tell Bob he is an ungrateful bastard, and he says he will stab my eyes out and eat my heart. Maybe the untold solitary years have made him madder."

Bronson spent some time in Broadmoor himself and claimed to know about the treatment of the criminally insane. He says the doctors recognized that he wasn't mad and, in the end, had no choice but to move him back to a high-security prison.

> "But Bob lives in a complete fantasy world of violence. We now hate each other. I pray to one day bump into him at 300mph, and, unlike him, I don't need a blade. Nobody rips my heart out or eats my brain – especially a fucking nutcase like Bob Maudsley."

Despite the animosity between them, there seems a world of difference between Maudsley and Bronson. For one thing, Charles Bronson has never killed anyone. And today, he acknowledges the violence of his past:

> "What I did was terrible. I was violent, and I hurt a lot of people. And I am truly sorry for that."

Maudsley did write a statement for Bronson's trial. His written statement was the poem "Not enough man hugs in this insane world."

During Bronson's trial, the prosecution claimed that Bronson had been waiting to target the governor, Mr. Docherty, for months in revenge for not releasing the 22 photos that were taken during his wedding. The court heard during the trial that Mr. Docherty suffered from swelling to the neck, scratches to his face, and whiplash following the attack from Bronson. Bronson was waiting outside of Docherty's office, whistling the *Great Escape* theme, and charged him as soon as he came out of his office.

The jury also heard the recording of Bronson's comment to the governor about biting his nose off, which was caught on one of the guard's body cams. Bronson said that they were just words, and he would never really go through with it:

> "It was a figure of speech. I would never dream of biting someone's nose off. I am a vegetarian and would never eat meat."

Born Gordon Michael Peterson on December 6, 1952, Charles Bronson was first sent to prison in 1974, when he was 22years old, for an armed robbery of a post office. For that offense, he was given seven years in prison. But the sentence was extended due to his attacks on prison guards and other inmates.

The first prison he was sent to was Walton Gaol, where he ended up in the punishment block within two weeks for attacking two other inmates without provocation. He was transferred to Hull Prison in 1975 and was given a job in the workshop. In the first week, he decided that he didn't want to work and refused to do anything. The guards forced him to go to the workshop, but instead of going to work, he started smashing up the shop.

It took five prison guards to break Bronson from his rampage and a sedative injection to get him under control. Again, he was sent to the punishment block and given an additional six-months on his sentence. After he recovered and was back in the general population, he remained hard to get along with and a problematic inmate. Not only for the guards but the other inmates. He was sent to solitary confinement at least once a month.

About six months into his sentence, he attacked another inmate, John Henry Gallagher, with a glass jar causing severe damage to the man's face. Charged with grievous bodily harm, and later convicted of the lower crime, unlawful wounding, Bronson had another nine months added to his sentence.

He transferred to Armley Gaol Prison, where he finally realized he had a reputation as a highly dangerous inmate. Everyone at the new prison knew who he was before he got there. Bronson loved the attention he was getting, so he kept up the violent attacks of guards and inmates as well as damaging prison property.

The Prison Authority moved Bronson several more times between different prisons (Wakefield, Parkhurst, Walton, and Armley) for the next two years. They were trying to find one that could keep him in line and get him to follow the rules. While he was in Parkhurst, he started a commotion in the lunchroom with some of the guards, and they ended up beating Bronson so bad he ended up in the hospital. During his recovery, he received divorce papers from his wife.

The next prison he was sent to was Wandsworth, but that didn't last more than a few months. He tried to poison the prisoner in the cell next to him. So, he was sent back to Parkhurst and put in the psychiatric ward, with the infamous Kray Twins. Bronson called the twins the best two guys he had ever met. He was put in solitary confinement after threatening to kill a nurse, doctor, and prison guard.

Bronson went back into the general population after his four-month term in solitary but was caught digging through his cell wall in an attempt to escape prison. So, back to solitary confinement, he went for another four months. As soon as he got out, he found the other inmate who told the guards about his plan to escape and beat him so severely the inmate was scarred for life.

Bronson continued his stretch of terror by attacking another prisoner with a jam jar and was again charged with grievous bodily harm. When they tried to arrest him, he assaulted a guard. Back in solitary confinement, he attempted to kill himself and was sectioned under the Mental Health Act and sent to Broadmoor Hospital for the Criminally Insane in December of 1978.

It was while Bronson was in the hospital that he attempted to strangle child sex murderer John White and was stopped just as White was giving out his death rattle. Bronson later said in his 2000 memoir, *Bronson*, that he could not relate to the other prisoners held in Broadmoor:

"I witnessed them running into walls, using their heads as rams. I've seen them fall unconscious doing this. They stabbed themselves with pens, needles, scissors. One even blinded himself in one eye, and another tore out his own testicle. There was one just kept trying to eat himself, biting his arms, legs, and feet."

Bronson was finally released from that charge in 1987, making it a total of 13 years served for a 7-year sentence because of his bad behavior. Once released, he started a career in bare-knuckle boxing. His promoter at the time thought he would do better if he had a catchy name, so he changed it to Charles Bronson, after the American actor.

Only one year later, in 1988, Bronson was back in jail. This time for planning another robbery. In prison, he would behave as badly as he had the first time, attacking other inmates, and even holding three people as hostages during confrontations with the guards.

Bronson has written many books about his experiences in prison and famous prisoners he met while incarcerated. He calls himself a fitness fanatic because of the many years he spent in solitary confinement. He dedicated a book to exercising in small spaces.

In 2014, he changed his name again to Charles Salvador, after the designer Salvador Dali, in an attempt to distance himself from the violent reputation he had under the Bronson name. He also created the Charles Salvador Art Foundation to help promote his artwork and help those in positions even less fortunate than his own.

CROSSBOW CANNIBAL: STEPHEN GRIFFITHS

Serial killer Stephen Shaun Griffiths was born on December 24, 1969, in Dewsbury, Yorkshire, England. In May 2010, he was arrested and charged with the Bradford murders, the murders of three sex workers in the city of Bradford in 2009 and 2010. He was convicted, sentenced to life in prison, and remanded to Wakefield Prison, aka "Monster Mansion."

On Monday, June 22, 2009, 43-year-old Susan Rushworth was last seen getting off of a bus near her apartment in Oak Villas. Rushworth was the mother of three, who struggled with epilepsy and was receiving treatment for heroin addiction. She also worked as a sex worker. The day she went missing, the police figured she was looking for drugs.

On Monday, April 26, 2010, 31-year-old Shelley Armitage left her apartment in Allerton with a friend to go for dinner and to do some shopping. Her friend left Armitage in the Bradford city center at about 10 p.m. that evening. Unfortunately, Armitage would not be seen again. She never showed up to claim her social welfare benefits, and she never used her cell phone after that night.

On Friday, May 21, 2010, a third person, 36-year-old Suzanne Blamires from Allerton, Bradford, disappeared.

The following Tuesday, May 25th, female body parts turned up in the River Aire in Shipley, near Bradford, West Yorkshire. On May 28th, the remains were confirmed to be that of Suzanne Blamires. Later that year, human tissue was found by police in the same river, and it was determined to belong to Shelley Armitage. No remains of Susan Rushworth were ever found.

Police also found suitcases that contained the tool used to dissect the bodies.

It was by accident that police found CCTV from the landlord of the apartment building in which Griffiths lived. The film showed Griffiths attacking Blamires. When they picked up Griffiths for questioning, he admitted to killing all three of the women. After the arrest, he went on to say that he actually had killed loads of women:

"I'm Osama Bin Laden."

Griffiths invited the women over to his place by offering them money for sex. The CCTV footage showed the women running from his apartment, and Griffiths chasing them, attacking them, and dragging them back to his apartment. He then shot the women with a crossbow and held his middle finger up to the camera. Further evidence included blood belonging to each of the victims found on the carpet in Griffiths' apartment.

Griffiths told officers he had eaten some of each of the girls, as that was part of the magic.

Stephen Griffiths was convicted on December 21, 2010, and sentenced to life in prison with no chance for parole. There was no evidence produced that could link Griffiths to any other crimes. Griffiths showed no remorse and appeared not only happy but very proud during his sentencing.

Griffiths had spent the previous six years getting a psychology degree and was now taking part-times courses at Bradford University, comparing 19th century and modern murder techniques. He set up a website called *The Skeleton and the Jaguar*, which not only contained photographs of over 50 killers but had lots of pictures of his weapon of choice, the crossbow.

Griffiths also posted pictures of himself on his website, naked from the waist up, with bible quotes placed below them. Such as, Ezekiel 25:17.

"The path of the righteous man is beset on all sides."

You might remember this quote was used in Quentin Tarantino's movie *Pulp Fiction* during a gory execution scene. He also stated that:

> "Humanity is not merely a biological condition; it is also a state of mind. On that basis, I am a pseudo-human being at best. A demon at worst."

Griffiths really enjoyed having power. The women he encountered were easy prey for him, but even with his psychology degree, he was no match for the other prisoners at Wakefield Prison. Inmates like Bronson or Maudsley were not scared of Griffiths and didn't give him any chances to use any psychology on them. They were much more direct and had the "don't mess with me, or I'll fucking kill you" attitude.

Griffiths started to feel fear and stress like he never had before. He figured he would do much better in a hospital such as Broadmoor, so he created plans to get himself committed. The first step was to stop talking with his legal team. The next step was to go on a hunger strike. After neither of those had any effect, he decided he would pretend to try and commit suicide. None of his attempts were believable, and he remains in "Monster Mansion" to this day, dangerously close to Robert Maudsley.

DOCTOR DEATH

Also housed in "Monster Mansion" from the years 2000 to 2004 was the infamous serial killer doctor, Harold Shipman, a.k.a. "Dr. Death."

Harold Frederick Shipman was born in Nottingham, England, on January 14, 1946, to average working-class parents. When Shipman was 17-years old, his mother was diagnosed with terminal lung cancer. She requested that her doctor administer a lethal dose of morphine to her at home, as she couldn't take the pain. Shipman witnessed the hard death of his mother, which later became the (MO) modus operandi in his murders.

Three years later, in 1966, Shipman married Primrose May Oxtoby, and the couple had four children together. Shipman studied medicine at the Leeds School of Medicine and graduated in 1970. He began to work at the Pontefract General Infirmary on Pontefract, Yorkshire, and by 1974, became a general practitioner at the Abraham Ormerod Medical Center in Todmorden, West Yorkshire.

| Harold Shipman

Shipman first got into trouble with the law in 1975, when he was caught forging prescriptions of Demerol for his personal use. He was fined 500 pounds and had to take a rehabilitation course to continue his practice. Once clean, he took a position as a general practitioner at the Donneybrook Medical Center in Hyde, close to Manchester.

Shipman continued to work at that practice through the 1980s and became a surgeon in 1983. He was so successful in his field that he interviewed as a medical expert for several television news programs.

Shipman gained the attention of law enforcement once again in May 1998, when one of the employees at the medical center expressed concerns about the high rate of death and cremations among Shipman's patients. The police were unable to find enough evidence to press any charges against Shipman and abandoned the investigation.

In August the same year, a taxi driver, John Shaw, contacted the police and told them he suspected Shipman of killing 21 patients. Police decided to reopen the investigation against Shipman. They soon heard from Angela Woodruff, whose mother, Kathleen Grundy, had passed away in June. Suspiciously, her mother's doctor, Shipman, signed her death certificate and was also left 385,000 pounds from her mother's will.

Police exhumed the body of Kathleen Grundy, and an autopsy was performed. Traces of heroin, usually used for pain control in terminal patients, were found. Shipman told police that Grundy was a heroin addict and produced his medical files of Grundy from his computer. Police then examined his computer further and discovered that Grundy's journal had been filled in after her death.

Detectives searched Shipman's office and found the typewriter that had been used to write Grundy's will. This led to his arrest in September 1998.

Detectives then investigated other deaths that Shipman had certified and created a list of 15 people that were suspicious enough for them to investigate further. They would soon find a pattern of Shipman administering lethal doses of diamorphine, signing the patients' death certificates, and then falsifying medical records to indicate that they were in bad health, and that was the reason they died.

He was charged with 15 murders and began trial on October 5, 1999. By January 31, 2000, he was convicted on all 15 counts of murder and sentenced to serve the rest of his life in prison without the chance of parole.

Shipman has been the only doctor in British history to

be found guilty of murdering his patients. Both Shipman and his wife deny his guilt and argue that the scientific evidence used against him was wrong.

He was sent to Wakefield Prison to serve out his life sentence with all the other high-profile prisoners. On January 13, 2004, just under four years of being housed in Wakefield, Shipman hanged himself from his cell window, using his bedsheets.

His death would divide the country where some people were thrilled he was gone, while others were left wondering about how he died. Suspicions were rife about if he really did hang himself, or had somebody else killed him. Quite a few media outlets called for an inquiry into his death. Some suspected other inmates might have killed Shipman. They were also concerned about the prisoners' welfare in Wakefield.

Shipman's reason for suicide was never discovered, though there was one report from a probation officer who was told by Shipman that he had considered committing suicide once. Shipman's cellmate later told investigators that Shipman's wife had started to believe that her husband was guilty of the murders and sent him a letter asking him to confess everything to her. In 2005, an inquiry into Shipman's death ruled that his suicide could not have been predicted or prevented.

In January of 2001, the West Yorkshire Police led an investigation into Shipman's practice following his activities. By July 2002, the inquiry concluded that Shipman had killed at least 215 of his patients between 1975 and 1998, and claimed that there were many other suspicious deaths, but there could be no definite cause ascribed to Shipman. A total of 459 people died under his care. The inquiry also discovered that Shipman stole well over 10,000 pounds worth of jewelry, which they seized out of his garage.

THE YORKSHIRE RIPPER: PETER SUTCLIFFE

Peter William Sutcliffe was born on June 2, 1946, in Yorkshire, England. He was dubbed the "Yorkshire Ripper" by the press and public after being convicted of murdering 13 women and attempting to murder seven others between 1975 and 1980.

Sutcliffe has been dangerously close to Maudsley on two occasions. First, at Broadmoor Hospital for the Criminally Insane, and later in the solitary confinement wing at Wakefield Prison, where he is currently housed.

| *The Yorkshire Ripper*

Sutcliffe was married to Kathleen Francis and worked odd jobs, including that of a gravedigger. Francis had several miscarriages during their marriage, and as a result, lost the ability ever to have children. Sutcliffe would often avail of the services of female prostitutes, and quite often have bad experiences with them.

In 1969, a prostitute stole his money, and he went looking for her. During his search, he followed another prostitute into a garage and assaulted her with a rock by hitting her over the head with it. She was able to get the license plate of the car Sutcliffe drove away in and reported it to the police. Police interviewed him the next day but later released him after she changed her mind about pressing charges.

It was another six years before Sutcliffe committed another assault in the summer of 1975. On July 5th, Anna Rogulsky was walking alone on the street when suddenly she was attacked. Sutcliffe hit her over the head with a ball-peen hammer and slashed her stomach with a knife. When someone saw what was happening to the woman, they screamed and called the police. Sutcliffe ran away. Rogulsky survived her attack after several months in the hospital.

In August the same year, Sutcliffe assaulted another woman, Olive Smell, using the same method of attack - hitting her over the head and slashing her with a knife. Again, he was interrupted by a neighbor and left her alive.

Two weeks later, he attacked 14-year-old Tracy Browne by hitting her on the head several times. She fell to the ground, and he was about to stab her when the headlights of a car shown directly on them, so he ran again. Tracy was alive but had to have several brain surgeries. Sutcliffe managed to get away with committing all of these assaults but confessed to them in later years after he was arrested for other crimes.

In October 1975, Sutcliffe committed his first murder. He hit Wilma McCann, a mother of four, over the head with a hammer to knock her unconscious. This time, there were no interruptions as Sutcliffe stabbed his victim over 15 times, in her throat, chest, and abdomen until she died.

His next victim was 42-year-old Emily Jackson. Jackson was having money problems, so she started offering sexual favors to men in her van. She picked up Sutcliffe in January 1976, and the pair went to an abandoned building to have sex. Sutcliffe hit her over the head until she passed out, he then dragged her body into the field behind the building and stabbed her several times with a screwdriver. When he got up to walk away, he gave her body a good kick and left his boot print on her thigh.

Sutcliffe picked up 20-year-old Marcella Claxton on May 9th, in Leeds, when she was walking home from a party. When she got out of the car, he hit her over the head with a hammer, and she passed out. He left her there on the road alive. Luckily, she was found and rushed to the hospital. She was four months pregnant but lost her baby as a result of the attack. She later testified against Sutcliffe at his trial.

He continued his attacks through 1977 with Irene Richardson on February 5th, a prostitute he bludgeoned to death with a hammer and mutilated with a knife. Then on April 29th, he killed Patricia Atkinson, a prostitute, in her apartment. On June 26th, he murdered 16-year-old Jayne MacDonald, who was out for a walk. On October 1st, 1977, he murdered Jean Jordan, a prostitute from Manchester, and then on December 14th, he attacked another prostitute named Marilyn Monroe, who survived and was later able to testify against him.

In 1978, Sutcliffe killed three more women who were prostitutes. In January, he murdered 21-year-old Yvonne Pearson and stuffed horsehair from a discarded sofa in her mouth. In February, his victim was 18-year-old Helen Rytka, and on May 16th, he killed Vera Millward.

In 1979, it would be another year of brutal killings for Sutcliffe. On April 4th, 19year-old Josephine Whitaker was walking home from work when she met her end at the hands of Sutcliffe, and on September 1st, 20-year-old Barbara Leach, a Bradford University student met hers. Because both victims in 1979 were not prostitutes, the murders started to cause panic around the community.

In April 1980, Sutcliffe was arrested for drunk driving and released on bond to await trial. While he was out, he killed two more women: 47-year-old Marguerite Walls on August 20th and 20-year-old Jacqueline Hill on November 17th. He attacked three other women that year, but all of them survived and were able to testify against him when he was finally on trial.

Sutcliffe picked up a 24-year-old prostitute Olivia Reivers on January 2, 1981. Police pulled him over because the license plates on the car he was driving did not match the vehicle's registration. He was arrested and taken to jail. When the police went back to the spot where he was arrested to check out the car, they found the knife and hammer in the back seat. Police then got a search warrant to inspect his house and brought Sutcliffe's wife in for questioning too.

Later, police strip-searched Sutcliffe and found he was wearing a V-neck sweater inverted under his pants. The sleeves were pulled over his legs, and the V-neck exposed his genitals. The sexual implications of his outfit were obvious to the police, and they spent the next two days intensely questioning Sutcliffe. He finally admitted that he was the Yorkshire Ripper.

Over the next day, Sutcliffe described all of his attacks very calmly to the police, like he was exchanging cooking recipes. Sutcliffe tried to claim the voice of God sent him on a mission to kill prostitutes. However, it was eventually discovered a lot of the women he murdered were not prostitutes. He was formally charged on January 5th.

At his trial, Sutcliffe pleaded not guilty to 13 charges of murder, and seven charges of attempted murder, but guilty to manslaughter on the grounds of diminished responsibility. The defense claimed that he was a tool of God's will who ordered him to kill these women. He claimed the voices originated from the headstone of a Polish man, Bronislaw Zapolski, and that they were of God.

The prosecution ordered a psychiatric evaluation of Sutcliffe, and four different psychiatrists diagnosed him with paranoid schizophrenia, so they felt it would be best to accept his plea. The judge in the case rejected the prosecution's request and ordered that Sutcliffe face a criminal trial with a jury.

The trial started on May 5, 1981, and lasted about two weeks. Sutcliffe was found guilty of all 13 charges of murder and seven charges of attempted murder. He was sentenced to 20 concurrent sentences of life imprisonment. He was also ordered to spend a minimum of 30 years in prison before being eligible for a parole hearing.

Following his conviction, Sutcliffe changed his last name to his mother's maiden name, Coonan. He began his incarceration at Parkhurst Prison. While there, he was assaulted by fellow prisoner James Costello. Costello broke a glass coffee pot onto Sutcliffe's face, causing 30 stitches around his eye.

In March of 1984, Sutcliffe transferred to Broadmoor Mental Hospital for the Criminally Insane as he was certified by the Mental Health Act in 1983. This was where he first came into contact with Robert Maudsley.

Sutcliffe was attacked continuously in Broadmoor by several different inmates, all claiming that he was a rapist and deserved to die. Ian Kay attacked him with a pen, stabbing out both his eyes. As a result, Sutcliffe lost the vision in his left eye completely, and partially in his right eye.

In February of 2009, Sutcliffe was classified fit to leave Broadmoor hospital and return to prison. He was sent to Wakefield Prison, where again, he met up with Maudsley.

The guards keep him in Wakefield's solitary confinement wing for his protection. He will serve out the rest of his sentence there close to Robert Maudsley.

Other notable criminals held in Wakefield Prison's solitary confinement wing with Maudsley include:

RICHARD BAKER

Baker was called "Britain's worst serial rapist" after his 1999 conviction of 13 rapes, and three attempted rapes. He is serving four life sentences without the chance of parole. In 2006, he was caught planning to escape from Wakefield. Maps and sketches were found hidden in his cell, earning him additional years to his sentence. His first meeting with Maudsley came after he was caught in the attempt to escape and was sent to the solitary confinement wing.

DAVID HARKER

Harker was convicted of killing and dismembering Julie Paterson, a mother of four. He admitted to eating pieces of her flesh with his pasta dinner. In 1999, he was sentenced to a minimum of 14 years. A mild punishment but fitting when claiming diminished responsibility. Harker was sent to serve his sentence in Wakefield and ended up in solitary confinement beside Maudsley after an attempt on his life. Alan Parker, his victim's boyfriend hell-bent on killing Harker, actually committed murder so he would be sent to Wakefield to avenge Julie.

IAN HUNTLEY

In 2003, Ian Huntley was charged and convicted of the murders of two 10-year-old girls, Holly Wells and Jessica Chapman. He was sentenced to life with a minimum of 40 years to be served before a chance of parole. He has been in Wakefield Prison since 2008 and in the solitary confinement wing with Maudsley the whole time. As a child killer, his life is always in danger.

SIDNEY COOKE

Sidney Cooke is the notorious pedophile with the nickname "Hissing Sid." He is serving two life sentences in Wakefield after sexual abuse convictions against two young boys.

He had a previous conviction of manslaughter on 14-year-old Jason Swift. He was sent to the solitary confinement wing with Maudsley after his life was threatened several times.

ROY WHITING

Whiting was convicted of the abduction and murder of 8-year-old Sarah Payne in 2001. He was sentenced to life imprisonment with a minimum of 40 years before a chance of parole. He was sent to Wakefield, where he was stabbed in a vicious attack by fellow inmates and needed emergency surgery to keep him alive. After he recovered, he was sent to the solitary wing with Maudsley, where he has been ever since.

IAN WATKINS

One of the other most famous 'monsters' in the mansion at Wakefield is the singer from the band Lost Prophets, Ian Watkins. In 2013, he was sentenced to 35 years and sent to Wakefield Prison after child sexual assault convictions, including the attempted rape of a baby. Not only was he in danger in prison because of his sexual assaults of children, but he was also a celebrity. Thereby making him a target for other prisoners thinking they could make themselves famous by being the one to kill him. Watkins was sent to the solitary wing and became friends with child killer Mick Philpott.

MARK HOBSON

Mark Hobson was convicted of killing his girlfriend and her twin, as well as two others in 2006, and sentenced to whole life without the possibility of parole to be served in Wakefield. In 2012, he was sent to the solitary wing after he attacked fellow inmate Ian Huntley with a pot of boiling water in the kitchen.

MICHAEL SAMS

Michael Sams was convicted in 1993 on several charges of blackmail and extortion, as well as the kidnapping and murder of Julie Dart and the kidnapping of Stephanie Slater. He was sentenced to four life sentences to be served at Wakefield Prison. In 1997, he was sent to solitary confinement as well as given an additional eight years on his sentence for holding a female probation officer hostage with a metal spike.

MARK BRIDGER

Mark Bridger was convicted of the abduction and murder of 5-year-old April Jones and sentenced to life imprisonment without the chance of parole. He was sent to Wakefield Prison, and within the first week, his face was slashed with a knife by a fellow inmate. He requested to be moved from the prison, but the request was denied. He was sent to the solitary confinement wing with Maudsley to serve out his term.

COLIN IRELAND

Colin Ireland was nicknamed the "Gay Slayer" after murdering at least five men he had targeted and picked up from gay pubs because they were gay. He was sentenced to life imprisonment and served out his sentence in Wakefield Prison until he died in 2012. He was attacked often, and some of the other inmates forced him to perform sexual favors for them. Ireland was not gay; instead, he wanted to kill gay people. But the prisoners assumed he was gay, and that was the reason for his crimes. He was in solitary confinement quite often because of the attacks he endured.

LEVI BELLFIELD

Levi Bellfield was convicted of three murders and one attempted murder in 2008. His murder victims were Amelie Delagrange, Marsha McDonnell, and 13-year-old Milly Dowler, and attempted murder victim was Kate Sheedy. He was sentenced to whole life imprisonment and will never be free. After he was incarcerated for about two years, he told the police that he committed several other murders and would confess to them. When the police checked on the murders he reportedly committed, they found him to be untruthful. He was sent to spend the rest of his life in Wakefield Prison.

LETTER TO THE TIMES UK

In September 2014, Eve-Ann Prentice released letters she had exchanged with Robert Maudsley. Below are a few excerpts from the article in *Forensic Psychology* on September 2, 2014:

> "How did I find myself in permanent solitary confinement at Wakefield? I first killed a man outside and found myself in Broadmoor. I then killed a fellow patient at Broadmoor and eventually found myself to Wakefield, where I killed two fellow inmates.
>
> It is on record that I served numerous periods of solitary confinement at Broadmoor prior to my killing a fellow patient, it is also on record I underwent a long period of solitary confinement in various prisons prior to my arrival at Wakefield and placement on normal location, at no time in

Broadmoor or those prisons did I receive any kind of psychological or psychiatric assistance or help.

Numerous national newspapers and tabloids have labelled me "Britain's own Hannibal Lecter." All very sensational, no doubt, and I have received numerous letters from people over the years who have watched this film Silence of the Lambs and who believe it is a genuine portrayal of my life story. They are, of course, entitled to their beliefs; however, a more accurate portrayal would be a film called Murder in the First.

I mention this because an important question for these people to ask would be, to what extent my conditions and environment and treatment at Broadmoor and HMP

Wakefield played in causing me to react in such a savage manner?

As you know, I don't see any psychologists nor any psychiatrists currently. It seems Wakefield is happy to place me in permanent solitary confinement after killing two of its prisoners. Actually, all of Wakefield has sought to do since 1978 is to demonize me.

Are we not all products of our environment, yourself, Ms. Prentice, and myself? Do we all not form our opinions, beliefs, etc. from how we perceive that environment? Wakefield prison authorities perceive me as a problem, their solution to that problem to date has been in effect to bury me alive, the cage ultimately for them being my concrete coffin, but is that the final solution?

What purpose is being served by keeping me

locked up for 23 hours a day? Why even bother to feed me and to give me an hour exercise a day, month, and year, yet not allow me to talk to any other inmate via their windows? Who am I actually a risk to?

Let me try to briefly answer that by saying I killed rapists, pedophiles and sex offenders, no other type of person nor type of offender, so my past crimes strongly suggest this is the group most solely at risk. Why is this? I can say that yes, I have been raped, and yes, I have been sexually abused, and consequently, I do detest these people enough to have killed them in the past. So, we have these circumstances from my childhood and adolescence.

I have no previous convictions for killing officers, and I have no previous convictions for seriously wounding nor stabbing any prison officers, and I cannot perceive, nor can I imagine any situation in which this could arise. I am left to stagnate, vegetate, and to regress, and left to confront my solitary head-on, with people that have eyes but don't see, and who have ears but don't hear, who have mouths but don't speak.

Consequently, I, too, am left with no voice, and the question I would ask of everyone at Wakefield is, why treat me the way they are? Why can't I listen to beautiful classical music? It may interest you to know that I am not even allowed a telephone or to write to The Mental Health Association, nor the Samaritans, if only for someone to talk to and express my concerns.

As far as I can see, because of my current

treatment and confinement, I feel that all I must look forward to is indeed psychological breakdown, mental illness, and, indeed, probable suicide. While inmates such as I am provided with nothing from the prison authorities, then accordingly, we are free of any responsibility whatsoever and thus can choose to act; however, our consciences dictate, opening our feelings of anger, hate, frustration, and ultimately hopelessness.

Inmates of Woodhill Control Unit are currently adequately demonstrating this on a daily basis. Will it take the possible death of other inmates or prison officers in that unit before the authorities address such an issue? I hope not.

Why can't I have a television in my cell to see the World and learn? Why can't I have any music tapes and listen to beautiful classical music? Why can't I have a budgie (similar to a Canary) instead of flies and cockroaches and spiders I currently have?

I promise to love it and not eat it. Why can't I have amazing pictures on my walls in solitary rather than dirty, damp patches I currently have? Why can't I possess or purchase postage stamps so I can maintain contact with my family, friends, and people who contact me?

If the prison authorities say no, then I ask for a simple cyanide capsule, which I shall willingly take, and the problem of Robert John Maudsley can easily and swiftly be resolved. Thank you."

The letter was signed by RJ Maudsley prisoner #467637 and appeared on *Reuters News Wire*, London, March 23, 2000. Several responses were made throughout every major press in the U.K., including *BBC TV*, *The Sunday Times*, and *Reuters*.

The following response to the above letter appeared courtesy of *Reuters News Wire*, London, March 23, 2000, with a spokesman from Prisoner's Services dismissing Maudsley's appeal:

> "Prisoners live in decent conditions, but we have to bear in mind security and control restrictions. You have to remember that Robert Maudsley was convicted of his first killing in 1974 and went on to kill three more people while in prison. He killed two of them in one afternoon, earning him the nickname "Hannibal the Cannibal" after author Thomas Harris' literary creation of Dr. Hannibal Lecter.
>
> Psychiatrists deemed Maudsley untreatable on the first murder, and the following murders he was convicted and sentenced in the normal criminal system."

Maudsley sent a letter to *The Sunday Express* in 2002, and it was later published in one of their articles about living inside a cage in solitary confinement:

> "At 8 a.m., breakfast is brought to my cage by my

keepers and put under the inner gate, which has a gap at the bottom. It consists of cornflakes, a carton of prison milk, a one-inch container of jam and one of butter, two bread rolls, and a bottle of hot water.

The milk is often sour, so I throw it and the corn flakes down the toilet and just eat the rolls with a cup of tea. This is the time I make applications to write letters or visiting orders. It is also the time I must request exercise. If I forget to ask, I am deemed not to need it.

If I have asked for exercise, six or seven officers take me out of the cage at 8:30 a.m. First, I stand on a wooden box and spread my arms; then, I am required to open my mouth, then stick out and lift my tongue. A keeper then gives me a rub down, while another keeper uses a metal detector all over my body. I have to lift my feet for inspection.

If I disagree with any aspect of this procedure, I am returned to my cage and deemed to have refused exercise. Exercise is for one hour. I am not allowed to smoke or bring anything to drink out into the exercise yard. If another inmate attempts to speak to me from his cell window, he could be given cellular confinement.

The yard has CCTV cameras and is made of concrete or Tarmac. There are no trees, grass, or flowers. It is bare, sterile, and bleak. I find the enforced silence depressing. When the hour is up, I have to go through the search process and return to the cage. I leave my shoes outside the cage. From 9:30-11 a.m., I see no one.

At 11 a.m., lunch is placed through the gap. I

usually only eat half as it is tasteless, bland, and unwholesome. At this time, I am usually given any mail and a prison newspaper.

At 5:50 p.m., I am given the last meal of the day. I am given hot water to last until 8 a.m. I am given two loaves of white sliced bread a week. This usually goes moldy after a few days. No extra butter or jam is provided.

On Wednesday afternoons my keepers bring me my canteen to the cage. These goods are from the prison shop. Usually, I can only afford hand-rolled tobacco, plus cigarette papers and a large box of matches.

On Sundays, I am meant to be given kit change. If it happens, I get one pillowcase, two sheets, two towels, two pairs of socks, two pairs of underpants, two T-shirts, and a set of one-piece overalls. If it doesn't happen, I have to stay in dirty clothes and sheets for another week."

EPILOGUE

Robert Maudsley has now been given a television for his cell, as well as a Sony PlayStation 2. According to his nephew Gavin Maudsley in *The Sun Times*, Robert loves to play the game *Call of Duty* so much that he turns down the single hour of exercise that he is allowed so that he can remain in his cage and play. Gavin is related to Robert Maudsley through his father Paul, Robert's brother:

> "My uncle does not want to leave solitary confinement, and he has no wish to be released from prison. He lives in his own little world. He's got his TV and his music and his PlayStation 2, with his favorite game Call of Duty. He tells me he is content with his life, and he does genuinely seem happy. He accepts he is going to die in jail, and he has no problem with that. He says there are so many bad people in the real world that he would rather be on his own."

Gavin Maudsley also revealed that his uncle was in a furious fight with another high-profile Wakefield prisoner, Charles Bronson. It started when Bronson tried to befriend him and get him to testify for him on a charge, and Robert refused:

> "I can often hear Charlie Bronson when I go visit my uncle as they are held in the same wing. They cannot see each other, but they communicate by shouting. They have times when they are okay and times when they're enemies. They have arguments because Charlie is such a nutter (in the UK, this word is often used to describe a person with psychotic behavior) and is always badgering him (Maudsley) by asking him to team up with him.
>
> Charlie once sent him a watch, telling a guard to give it to him. My uncle said, "I'm never getting out, what do I want a watch for? Give it back." Charlie got offended, then started shouting, "I'm going to kill you when I see you." But Maudsley shouted back, "You've never killed anyone, you soft cunt." This was a few years ago.
>
> Another time Charlie went to the gym and left his trademark John Lennon sunglasses in there. Uncle Bob went in afterward and took them. So, the next thing I knew, Charlie was suing Wakefield Prison for 250 pounds. I think he gave them back eventually by handing the glasses to a guard and told him to tell Charlie to stick them up his arse."

Gavin continues:

> "My uncle tells me what keeps him going is his determination to beat the system that has allowed him to be in solitary for over 40 years now. He gave up smoking because it was one of the ways they would mess with him. They used to wave tobacco in his face, laugh at him and tell him he wasn't going to get any. After that, he told me they started spitting in his food. He seems to be treated better now that he has outlived most of the wardens who hated him."

Robert Maudsley is still escorted with no less than six guards anytime he does leave his cell. His cell is still the two small cages, covered by bulletproof glass, and he still sleeps on the bed slab bolted to the cement floor. Most of the guards are still very scared of him. Perhaps it's the fact that he is named after "Hannibal the Cannibal?" Gavin explains:

> "Uncle Bob thinks his nickname is stupid, considering he never ate anyone, it's just that he smashed in one victim's skull so badly it looked like part of his brain was missing. But some of the guards still buy into this idea that he can snap their heads with two fingers. Others don't believe it,

and he even has the odd game of chess with them."

In the summer of 2017, Maudsley's security relaxed some, enough for him to attack a guard who had spit in his food. Instead of shoving the food tray under the cell through the little slot used for giving things to Maudsley, the guard opened the cell door and handed the tray of food to him. Maudsley then smashed the tray over the guard's head. According to Gavin:

"Robert was angry because they'd put this crazy person on his wing, and he's spent the night screaming and keeping everyone awake. Attacking the guard was the only way he could make his voice heard, but I don't think he hurt him too badly. He told me, come on, it was only a plastic tray."

Gavin also stated that his uncle gets the flu now and again, and recently had a tooth removed. He is getting older now and has short gray hair. He used to keep his hair and nails very long, but because he was getting called "wolf-man," he decided to cut them.

In 2012, Maudsley became ill enough to require a doctor's visit twice a day, according to *The Daily Mirror*. The sickness was reportedly due to severe weight loss, and adverse side effects from the drugs he was taking for his mood swings.

The strangest thing of all is that Robert Maudsley

seems to be keeping himself alive intending to beat Albert Woodfox's record of having been the prisoner to be held in solitary confinement the longest. Woodfox was kept in solitary in a Louisiana, US jail for 43 years for the killing of a prison guard. When his nephew tells him that he has got to beat the world record, he will smile and nod.

Dr. Hugo Milne, a leading criminal psychologist who has spent many hours with other serial killers, including Peter Sutcliffe, "The Yorkshire Ripper," and Donald Neilson, "Black Panther," has admitted that

> "Maudsley was the only one I've ever been frightened of."

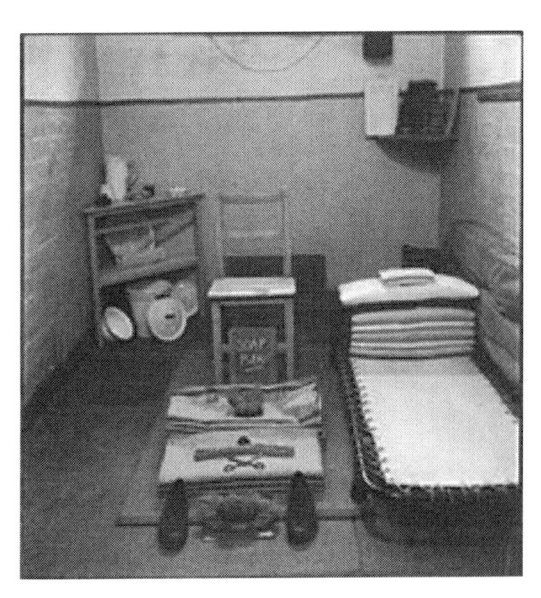

Prison Cell for Regular Inmates in Wakefield

ABOUT THE AUTHOR

Alan R. Warren has written several Best Selling True Crime books and has been one of the hosts and producer of the popular NBC news talk radio show 'House of Mystery' which reviews True Crime, History, Science, Religion, Paranormal Mysteries that we live with every day from a darker , comedic and logical perspective and has interviewed guests such as Robert Kennedy Jr., F. Lee Bailey, Aphrodite Jones, Marcia Clark, Nancy Grace, Dan Abrams and Jesse Ventura.

The show is based in Seattle on KKNW 1150 A.M. and syndicated on the NBC network throughout the United States including on KCAA 106.5 F.M. Los Angeles/Riverside/Palm Springs, as well in Utah, New Mexico, and Arizona.

ALSO BY

IN CHAINS: THE DANGEROUS WORLD OF HUMAN TRAFFICKING

Human trafficking is the trade of people for forced labor or sex. It also includes the illegal extraction of human organs and tissues. And it is an extremely ruthless and dangerous industry plaguing our world today.

Most believe human trafficking occurs in countries with no human rights legislation. This is a myth. All types of human trafficking are alive and well in most of the developed countries of the world like the United States, Canada, and the UK. It is estimated that $150 billion a year is generated in the forced labor industry alone. It is also believed that 21 million people are trapped in modern day slavery – exploited for sex, labor, or organs.

Most also believe since they live in a free country, there is built-in protection against such illegal practices. But for many, this is not the case. Traffickers tend to focus on the most vulnerable in our society, but trafficking can happen to anyone. You will see how easy it can happen in the stories included in "In Chains."

Amazon United States

Amazon Canada

Amazon United Kingdom

BEYOND SUSPICION: RUSSELL WILLIAMS: A CANADIAN SERIAL KILLER

Young girl's panties started to go missing; sexual assaults began to occur, and then female bodies were found! Soon this quiet town of Tweed, Ontario, was in panic. What's even more shocking was when an upstanding resident stood accused of the assaults. This was not just any man, but a pillar of the community; a decorated military pilot who had flown Canadian Forces VIP aircraft for dignitaries such as the Queen of England, Prince Philip, the Governor General and the Prime Minister of Canada.

This is the story of serial killer Russell Williams, the elite pilot of Canada's Air Force One, and the innocent victims he murdered. Unlike other serial killers, Williams seemed very unaffected about his crimes and leading two different lives.

Alan R. Warren describes the secret life including the abductions, rape and murders that were unleashed on an unsuspecting community. Included are letters written to the victims by Williams and descriptions of the assaults and rapes as seen on videos and photos taken by Williams during the attacks.

This updated version also contains the full brilliant police interrogation of Williams and his confession. Also, the twisted way in which Williams planned to pin his crimes on his unsuspecting neighbor.

Amazon United States

Amazon Canada

Amazon United Kingdom

REFERENCES

1. https://www.thesun.co.uk/news/4231452/hannibal-the-cannibal-uk-dangerous-prisoner/
2. https://www.theguardian.com/uk/2003/apr/27/ukcrime
3. https://groups.google.com/forum/#!topic/alt.true-crime/zFtr9tyFR5U
4. http://news.bbc.co.uk/2/hi/uk_news/687659.stm
5. https://www.mirror.co.uk/news/uk-news/cannibal-robert-maudsley-in-jail-plea-212791
6. https://www.manchestereveningnews.co.uk/whats-on/whats-on-news/conversations-serial-killer-paul-harrison-14404935
7. Wansell, Geoffrey: *Lifers*, June 9, 2016, Penguin ASIN: B015GLXPSQ.
8. Appleyard, Nick: *Life Means Life: Jailed Forever: True Stories of Britain's Most Evil Killers,* March 13, 2009, John Blake Publisher, ISBN: 1844546683.
9. https://www.lifedeathprizes.com/real-life-crime/

monster-mansion-hm-prison-wakefield-uks-notorious-jail-64494

10.   https://web.archive.org/web/20120313004617/http://www.pcc.org.uk/news/index.html?article=NTcxNw==

11.   https://www.liverpoolecho.co.uk/news/liverpool-news/tragic-life-led-hannibal-killings-3554260

Printed in Great Britain
by Amazon